3-D OPTICAL

✳ ILLUSIONS ✳

to

BAFFLE THE MIND

Jessica Rusick

Super Sandcastle

An Imprint of Abdo Publishing
abdobooks.com

abdobooks.com

Published by Abdo Publishing, a division of ABDO, PO Box 398166, Minneapolis, Minnesota 55439. Copyright © 2020 by Abdo Consulting Group, Inc. International copyrights reserved in all countries. No part of this book may be reproduced in any form without written permission from the publisher. Super SandCastle™ is a trademark and logo of Abdo Publishing.

Printed in the United States of America, North Mankato, Minnesota
102019
012020

THIS BOOK CONTAINS
RECYCLED MATERIALS

Design: Aruna Rangarajan, Mighty Media, Inc.
Production: Mighty Media, Inc.
Editor: Rachael Thomas
Design Elements: Shutterstock Images
Cover Photographs: Mighty Media, Inc., Shutterstock Images
Interior Photographs: Floriana/iStockphoto, p. 6; Gugurat/iStockphoto, p. 7 (geometric shape); Mighty Media, Inc., pp. 10, 11, 12, 13, 14, 15, 16, 17, 18, 19, 20, 21, 22, 23, 24, 25, 26, 27, 28, 29, 30 (top kid); Shutterstock Images, pp. 4, 5, 7, 8, 9, 11 (LEGO bricks), 12 (kid), 17 (kid), 18 (hand), 20 (kid), 22 (kid), 24 (kid), 29 (group of kids), 30; YOSHIKAZU TSUNO/Getty Images, p. 31
The following manufacturers/names appearing in this book are trademarks: LEGO®, Scotch®,

Library of Congress Control Number: 2019943343

Publisher's Cataloging-in-Publication Data
Names: Rusick, Jessica, author.
Title: 3-D optical illusions to baffle the mind / by Jessica Rusick
Description: Minneapolis, Minnesota : Abdo Publishing, 2020 | Series: Super simple magic and illusions
Identifiers: ISBN 9781532191626 (lib. bdg.) | ISBN 9781532178351 (ebook)
Subjects: LCSH: Magic tricks--Juvenile literature. | Sleight of hand--Juvenile literature. | Optical illusions--Juvenile literature. | Science and magic--Juvenile literature.
Classification: DDC 152.148--dc23

Super SandCastle™ books are created by a team of professional educators, reading specialists, and content developers around five essential components—phonemic awareness, phonics, vocabulary, text comprehension, and fluency—to assist young readers as they develop reading skills and strategies and increase their general knowledge. All books are written, reviewed, and leveled for guided reading and early reading intervention programs for use in shared, guided, and independent reading and writing activities to support a balanced approach to literacy instruction.

To Adult Helpers

The projects in this series are fun and simple. There are just a few things to remember to keep kids safe. Some projects require the use of sharp, hot, or chemical materials. Make sure kids protect their clothes and work surfaces. Review the projects before starting, and be ready to assist when necessary.

KEY SYMBOL

Watch out for this warning symbol in this book. Here is what it means.

HOT

You will be working with a hot object. Get help!

5/22

Contents

THE MAGIC OF
3-D Optical Illusions

Have you ever seen a shape that shouldn't exist? Or a dollar bill that smiles when moved a certain way? These are 3-D optical **illusions**!

THEN AND NOW

Since ancient times, scientists have noted how our brains are fooled by illusions. By studying illusions, scientists today can learn how our brains **interpret** the world.

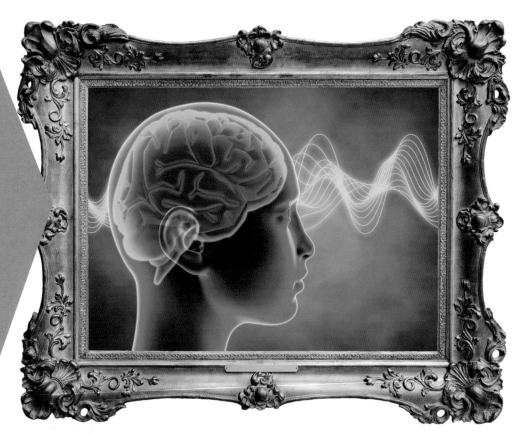

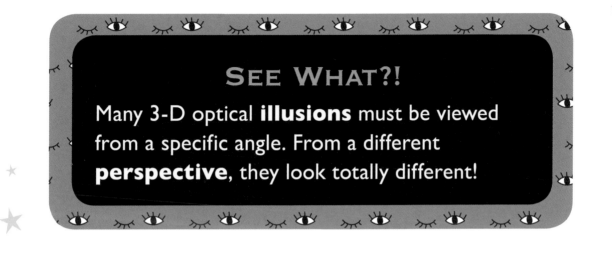

SEE WHAT?!

Many 3-D optical **illusions** must be viewed from a specific angle. From a different **perspective**, they look totally different!

Do you see a floating shape? ·······················▶ THINK AGAIN!

3-D optical **illusions** fool our senses. They can cause us to see things that aren't there. Or, illusions can make us miss things that are there. This seems like magic! But like all magic tricks, there are **techniques** and science behind each illusion.

The Möbius Strip is a famous illusion. It looks like it has two surfaces. But if you were to try drawing a line on both surfaces without lifting your pencil, you find there's only one!

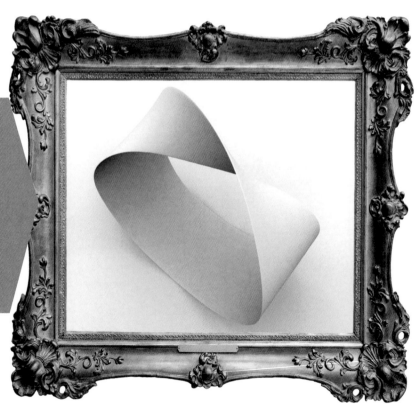

Tips and Techniques

Optical **illusions** trick the brain into seeing things differently from how they actually are. Discover the keys to making this type of magic work!

3-D optical **illusions rely** on **details**. A trick might depend on holding a **prop** at a **precise** angle. Or, the key could be standing at the right distance to hide something from the **audience**. One wrong move can make or break a 3-D optical illusion!

 1 Read the steps carefully.

2 Practice in front of a friend to figure out the best angle for a trick.

3 Come up with jokes and stories to **distract** your audience.

 Remember, the brain is smart! Tricking it takes precision.

PRACTICE AND PRESENTATION

Sometimes, your 3-D optical **illusion** might not work out. That's okay! Like all magic tricks, 3-D optical illusions take practice to get right.

Presentation is also important. Don't let your **audience** see you set up your trick. If an optical illusion must be viewed from a certain **perspective**, don't let your audience see it any other way!

3-D ILLUSIONIST

Tool Kit

Here are some of the materials that you will need for the tricks in this book.

QUARTER

CONSTRUCTION PAPER

DOLLAR BILL

LADLE

HOT GLUE GUN & GLUE STICKS

STYROFOAM RINGS

SCISSORS

SANDPAPER

LEGO BRICKS

RULER

CLEAR TAPE

Scotch

RING ROLL

Create a mesmerizing rolling illusion!

Materials

+ 2 Styrofoam rings of the same size
+ sandpaper
+ hot glue gun & glue sticks

Use sandpaper to create a flat area on a Styrofoam ring. Repeat this process with the second Styrofoam ring. Make the sanded surfaces the same size and angle for both rings.

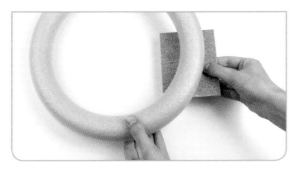

Put hot glue on the flat area of one ring.

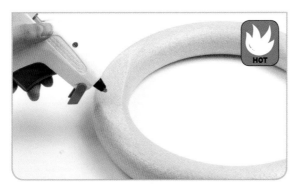

Press the flat area of the rings together. Let the glue dry.

Roll the rings on the floor for a cool 3-D **illusion**!

Amazing

TWO-HEADED COIN

Show your audience an impossible coin!

Materials
+ quarter

1   Point your index finger to the side and your thumb straight up.

2   Hold a coin by its edges between your index finger and thumb. Your thumb should be on top. Point the heads side of the coin toward you.

3   Press on the top of the coin with your thumb. Your thumb will want to slide down the back of the coin.

4   Quickly slide your thumb down the back of the coin.

5   At the same time, twist your wrist 180 degrees toward you. The coin's heads side will be facing up again!

6   With practice, this motion will become quick and fluid. Try it on multiple coins in a row to show off your two-headed coin collection!

FLOATING ORB

Make an orb
float between
your hands!

Materials

+ ladle
+ long-sleeved
  shirt with tight
  sleeves

1 Make sure your **audience** is in front of you. Keep the ladle hidden. Tell the audience that you will make a ball float in midair.

2 Turn your back to the audience. While turned, slip the ladle's handle into your sleeve.

3 Clasp your hands around the bowl of the ladle so it is covered.

4 Turn to face the audience. Open your hands to reveal the floating ball.

5 Turn back around and slip the ladle out of your sleeve. Or, reveal the ladle to make everyone laugh!

CHANGING FACES

Make your money smile and frown!

1 Place the bill in front of you. Make a **mountain fold** through the center of the face's left eye.

2 Unfold the bill. Make another mountain fold through the center of the face's right eye.

3 Unfold the bill. Make a **valley fold** between the two folds you already made. This third fold should be down the middle of the face's mouth.

4 Tug the ends of the bill slightly. You should be able to see the entire face, but the folds should still be there.

5 Show the bill's face to your **audience**. When you tilt it up, the face will appear to smile.

6 Slowly tilt the bill down. The smile will turn into a frown!

IMPOSSIBLE PAPER

Fold paper into an impossible shape!

1 Fold the paper in half lengthwise. Open the paper.

2 Find the halfway point along one long side of the paper. Cut inward at this point, stopping at the center **crease**.

3 Cut the other long side of the paper into thirds. Stop cutting when you reach the center crease.

4 Flip the paper over so the center crease folds up like a mountain. The side with one cut should be closest to you.

5 Fold the thirds back and forth to reinforce the creases.

6 Put your thumb on one end of the center crease. Flip one half of the paper 180 degrees toward you. One of the thirds should now be on the other side!

7 Crease the middle third. Flap it back and forth to show off your impossible paper!

MÖBIUS SQUARE

Change one shape into another!

Materials

- construction paper
- scissors
- ruler
- clear tape

1 Cut out two 8 x 1¼-inch (20 x 3 cm) paper strips.

2 Bend one strip into a ring. Tape the ends together.

3 Wrap the second strip through the ring. Tape the ends together. You should now have two rings that are joined.

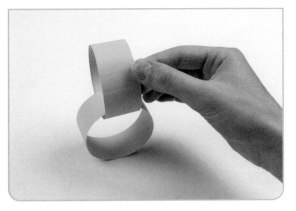

4 Add a small piece of tape where the rings meet. The rings should stay together without sliding.

5 Cut along the center of one ring, dividing it into two narrower rings. To do this, you will need to cut through the other ring. This creates two rings connected by a strip.

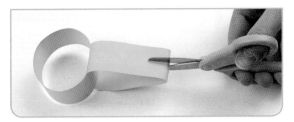

6 Cut down the middle of the strip.

7 Unfold your paper **illusion**. Your paper rings are now one Mobius Square!

IMPOSSIBLE TRIANGLE

Build a logic-defying shape!

Materials

+ eight 2 x 2 LEGO bricks

+ two 2 x 10 LEGO plates

+ two 2 x 4 LEGO bricks

+ one 2 x 8 LEGO brick

1 **Stack** seven 2 x 2 bricks on top of each other. Set them aside.

2 Stack two 2 x 10 plates on top of each other.

3 Place two 2 x 4 bricks and one 2 x 2 brick under the 2 x 10 stack.

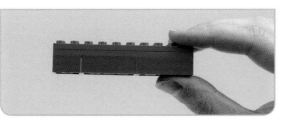

4 Put the 2 x 2 stack from step 1 on top of one end of the 2 x 10 stack from step 3. This will make an *L* shape.

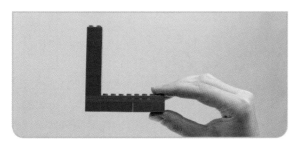

5 Put a 2 x 8 brick on top of the 2 x 2 stack. The 2 x 8 brick should be **perpendicular** to the 2 x 10 plate.

6 Turn the piece so that the ends look like they are connected to form a triangle. This is your **illusion**!

MAGIC TUBE

Pull objects from thin air!

Materials

+ two sheets of construction paper
+ clear tape
+ scissors
+ plastic flowers, ribbons, scarves, or other small objects

1 Before the trick, roll one sheet of paper lengthwise into a **cylinder**. Tape the edge down.

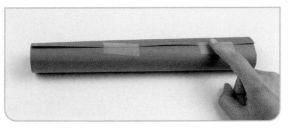

2 Roll the second sheet of paper lengthwise into a cone. One end of the cone should be about the same size as one end of the cylinder. The other end should be smaller. Tape the edge down.

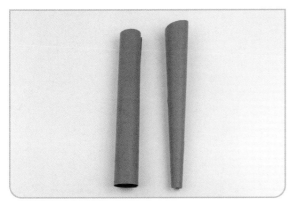

3 Put the small end of the cone into the cylinder.

4 Cut off the part of the cone that sticks out of the cylinder.

5 This creates a tube with a secret space. From one end, the tube looks empty. But on the other end, there is a place to hide things.

CONTINUED ON NEXT PAGE

6 Fill the secret space with plastic flowers, ribbons, or other small objects.

7 To perform the trick, have your **audience** look into the end of the tube with the smaller end of the cone. The tube will look empty.

8 After they've seen the "empty" tube, pull your objects out of the secret space.

Host a
MAGIC SHOW!

3D **illusions** need more than **props** and practice. They also require an **audience**! When you have a few illusions ready, put on a show for your friends and family. You could try setting up a stage for it. Or, keep it simple and gather your audience around a table.

Cool

Whoa

TIPS TO BECOME A
Master Illusionist

Be **confident** when **presenting** your **illusions**.

Keep each illusion's tricky elements a secret if you wish.

A little mystery makes magic fun!

ICONIC ILLUSIONIST

Kokichi Sugihara is a Japanese **mathematical engineer** known for creating "impossible objects." These objects are actually 3-D optical **illusions**! Sugihara's illusions **rely** on **perspective** to work. One of Sugihara's

best-known impossible objects is a white arrow that points to the right. When the arrow spins 180 degrees, it still seems to point to the right!

Glossary of Magic Words

audience – a group of people watching a performance.

confident – feeling sure you can do something.

crease – a line made by folding something.

cylinder – a solid, round shape with flat ends. A soda can is a cylinder.

detail – a small part of something.

distract – to cause to turn away from one's original focus of interest.

illusion – something that looks real but is not.

interpret – to explain or decide the meaning of something.

mathematical engineer – someone who solves engineering problems using math.

mountain fold – a fold in which the crease points up, like a mountain.

perpendicular – being at a right angle to a line or level.

perspective – how objects appear to the eye in respect to their distance and position.

precise – accurate or exact. The quality or state of being accurate or exact is precision.

present – to show or talk about something to a group or the public. A performance is called a presentation.

prop – an object that is carried or used by a performer in a performance.

rely – to depend on.

stack – to put things on top of each other.

technique – a method or style in which something is done.

valley fold – a fold in which the crease points down, like a valley.